M000310302

Pro... 1190 W. 900 N.
Provo, UT 84604
801-437-3100

Many Places

Written by Janet Kaderli

STECK-VAUGHN
ELEMENTARY · SECONDARY · ADULT · LIBRARY
A Harcourt Company

www.steck-vaughn.com

Towns have many different places.
People do a job at each place.

This is a place for many books.
Can you name this place?

This is a library.
Librarians work here.

This is a place for firetrucks.
Can you name this place?

This is a fire station.
Firefighters work here.

This is a place for sick people.
Can you name this place?

This is a hospital.
Doctors and nurses work here.

This is a place for mailing letters.
Can you name this place?

This is a post office.
Mail carriers work here.

This is a place to call for help.
Can you name this place?

This is a police station.
Police officers work here.

This is a place for children to learn.
Can you name this place?

This is a school.
Teachers work here.

This is a place for a family.
Can you name this place?

This is a home.
A family lives here!